2014

Sayyar Ismail

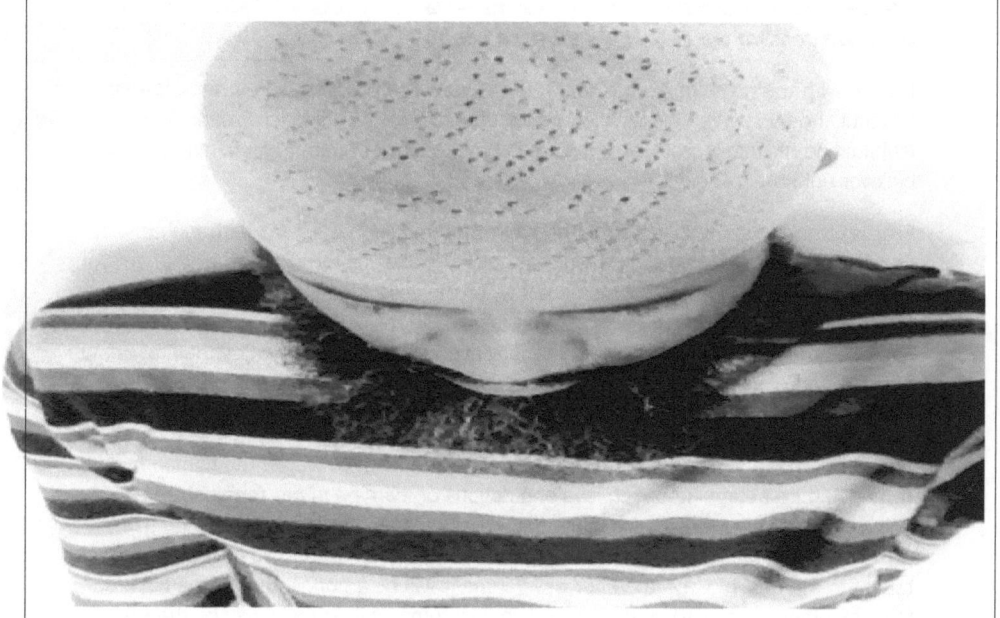

"FEAR"

What Are You Afraid Of...?

INTRODUCTION

Bismi-allah Ar'Rahman Ar'Rahim wa mursalan elay Rasoolullah salallahu alahi wa salaam wa alaa A'aleehi wa a'sahabihi thaweAtuwqa...

I begin with the name of Allah (Creator of heavens & earth) the Beneficent and most Merciful and by sending blessings of peace upon the last Messenger/Prophet Muhammad his family, companions and all Prophets from Adam to Muhammad & every believer until the last day.

Fear is often the emotion we forget about yet, on a daily basis it may arise in most of us only to be subsided by something that quickly makes us forgot. The car that cut you off causing you to lose control momentarily, or the child nearly hit, thrill rides at the amusement park...fear is to us something I think we really take for granite as an emotion and may not even consider in a positive way at all unless enjoy the first 90mph plunge on a roller coaster as it races towards the bottom. But how do you consider it In everyday life?

It's ironic, and in most cases grossly misunderstood just how fragile the human mind is. If the mind isn't stimulated with love and actions of learning in our formidable years between the ages of 1-7yrs the mind may not develop in the best way leaving many with disabilities of all sorts i.e. physical, mental, & societal; and if we are comforted and taught in the best of ways then our development will be amongst that of the best. But fear sometimes seems to be the hardest to overcome as it actually may be the source of a condition we possess. I want to lose weight, or stop smoking, go to college, move, or settle down get married...whatever the situation fear is usually at the base of what is stopping a person from carrying out the action. In yet other aspects fear can be an enhancement and come at a time that will give us that extra something we need to overcome. An attacker or crises situation people often tell stories of survival that if fear were not present within them they may not have had the strength or courage giving them the extra push of energy & stopping their lives short. This condition shouldn't to be mistaken for the presentation you need to give in front of the class or colleagues, and the clammy hands, higher pitched voice, and forehead perspiration showing on your now glossy face...This is nervousness and although it's close, it's not the same as fear. Nervousness comes as a condition sourced from ourselves often linked to confidence or in the example of public speaking, lack of confidence we contemplate before our performance; fear on the other hand is perceived from some external source. The desire of wanting to do well, and then second guessing our self's is a condition we are putting ourselves. Nonetheless both raise our awareness in the situation we are currently facing. But, what about societal fear? Yeah, we all know when we ourselves are fearful of something, but why or how is society made to fear. How can many different people, genders, different races, backgrounds etc. all be made to fear something? Easy...THE MEDIA!!!

You would be shocked to learn that millions of sharks are killed every year due to the release of the movie "Jaws" 30yrs ago...This movie, casting on the beaches of Massachusetts during the holiday season of the summer brought a lot of relative thought to beach goers. Since the area of the North Atlantic is known to have sharks, but few human accounts of personal attacks, it was a box office smash...the du du duuuuh music that accompanied the dorsal fin of the shark moving through the water has placed a 30yr psychological fear into millions of people young and old, man & woman. The power of the Media is without doubt unsurpassed by any military or power of money. The psychological ability to induce fear is such an effective weapon, that this movie has been a huge source of contribution to scientist and psychologist on the subject of fear. Hollywood has also masterminded the art of demonizing ethnic groups & images in order to conjure up fear or hatred in people towards these groups. I think anyone who has lived more than 50yrs now could surely witness the shift of villain images portrayed on the movie screen as well as the culture of fear in the world. What makes your daily news media any different???

Beyond the normal instinctive or innate fear we all have is the psychological fear of seeing images put before us on a frequent basis so much so that subconsciously we are being harmed and don't even realize it. Since fear is a human reaction that takes place in the brain towards outside threats and or entities this daily dose of frequent speech & use of imagery through media is certainly overcoming people on a daily basis. In fact, some of us fear things or people and we ourselves don't really understand why or how we have come to fear those things...But how else has feared governed our lives, altered our lives or influenced our lives? The age old conditioning of stereotypes and prejudices are really cemented into the very fabric of the country often only over looked in celebrity while the poor are still regard through the eyes of prejudice. Have you considered how fear has helped to alter laws, how it's shifted the culture of the populace? Everything is being driven on your fear...Besides the fear from the top you have fear you yourself need to overcome.

Sayyar Ismail Swift
Casablanca, Morocco
haqoverbatil@gmail.com

about [Number] words

"FEAR"

By

Order and fan based Email:
....haqoverbatil@gmail.com

Edited by: .... Sayyar Isma'il Swift

Corrections: .... Sayyar Isma'il Swift
Art:...Sayyar Isma'il Swift

Printed: .... USA, Canada & North Africa

TABLE OF CONTENTS

WHAT PEOPLE DON'T UNDERSTAND THEY TEND TO FEAR

The age old cliché' used to describe why people react to things they don't understand in a manner of fear... But is there any truth to this cliché' or is it just a cliché' at best? Personally I think it is true...Fear of the Unknown is really what this is. Uncertainty is a common motivation that stalls people all the time in fear towards something...Leaving a dead-end job, abusive marriage, major purchases, relocating etc. Doubtful or hesitant towards something is the condition many of us fall into when contemplating an action based from this type of fear. Not knowing what is waiting around the corner or what will be the consequences to the decision you act upon today. Well, life is full of uncertainty and there is absolutely no way to change this. Reading horoscopes or seeking the aid of some psyche friend is not going to give you any surety to the uncertainty we all face. The fabric of life is designed in this way...being that life is hidden from us in this way one would think that better actions would come from us all towards one another since we are completely in the dark as to what each of our fates have in store for us. But it's the exact opposite...We act out of selfishness, miserliness, arrogance, and desensitized ways all the time not realizing that LITTERALLY any second could be our last. The aspect of life offers us nothing, but what about things that do? In matters in which we could and should be aware are we? When something comes up in conversation or when your path crosses with someone different does this same fear rise up within you. If it does, have you asked yourself why, and have you tried to diagnose this issue for yourself? Many of us carry around with us dormant fears. Fear that is there but the person isn't aware that it is until the trigger to that fear is pulled. Isolation with someone different than yourself in an elevator, opposite sex or someone you have been paired up with in school or at work that you barely know anything about. Dormant until the time arises, so why not access this condition while it is present instead of waiting for the condition to pass allowing your fears to subside again until the next time? Some of these dormant fears may have actually been placed there by others and not by yourself. Have you ever noticed the fearlessness of children towards any and everything? Especially boys, you find them doing all sorts of things...Things adults wouldn't think of and we find ourselves fearful for them when we find them hanging from the top of trees, or holding onto the back of a truck in traffic while on their skateboard or worst. Children are also less scared when isolated, or paired up with people that are different. Learned behavior from observing their parents, a huge channel of passing on fears to children; other ways are by speech and teaching them prejudices and stereotypes etc. Children may live their entire younger years unaware of certain fears they have until they reach high school or in some cases college where the melting pot of ethnicity broadens from the sheltered confines of their small towns/cities. Faced with these fears for the first time, we have to now realize how they got there in the first place and address them right away so we know longer fear what is not necessary. This would be the correct manner in eradicating the fear of something you don't understand...why would you want to remain fearful of something when for the most part all you have to do is ask, come into the know about that in which you are ignorant. In a 2005 Gallop poll in the United States children between ages of 13-15 were asked what they feared the most the top 10 were the following: Terrorist attack, Spiders, Death, Being a failure, War, Criminal or gang violence, Being alone, The future, and Nuclear War. In another interesting survey book author Bill Tancer analyzed the most frequent search criteria on the internet in regards to fear and he found the following top flying, heights, clowns, intimacy, death, rejection, people, snakes, failure and driving; the age group was not included in the analysis.

Fear either cripples us or it enables us. When fear cripples us, we are literally at the mercy of the fear of that person, place or thing which is the source of the fear. Much like not being in control of yourself or your actions while under the influence of some narcotic or alcohol...Losing this control of ourselves is servitude towards that which has taken us...in other words the things we fear we are slaves too in one aspect. Why won't the slave try to escape? Fear!!! Fear of being caught and beaten then treated worse than he or she had been treated before or even killed. So the simple reminder of the thing they feared was enough to keep many in service to their masters. If we are also crippled by some sort of fear in our lives or some misunderstanding we are giving up a lot in terms of freedom. Fearing what you don't understand, and hating what you can't conqueror...Both mindsets are conditions to passiveness towards one's own state; therefore a hatred is derived out of that same condition born from ourselves. Basically to overcome something we first have to understand that in which we are to overcome. Everyone should be the best in auditing themselves; but how many still seek to ignore major issues about themselves and seek opinions from others? It's as though they are hoping for a medical condition or something else to shift the blame to instead of coming to the starting realization that it is YOU!!! Two warring armies are obligated to understand each other if they are to be successful in winning. In the old days, it wasn't uncommon for two leaders, generals, or kings etc. to meet face to face to promote diplomacy; but while having dialogue they were sizing each other up trying to understand each other mentally. Thus understanding ones' opponent on a more intimate level might give them insight to how they may think or decided when contemplating fatal maneuvers. On this notion fear that can be used would therefore be rational verses that in which cripples to be something irrational. Rational fear heightens the senses, and gives oneself a boost or rush. We see this with all the base jumpers, and bungee cord, mountain dew types...all seeking that rush of adrenaline that only fear can bring about. Irrational fear is said to be a phobic type...A phobia defined to be a persistent, irrational fear of something, activity, or situation that leads someone to avoid it at all cost. This irrational type of fear is very deep rooted, but usually remains because it is avoided at all cost instead of dealt with. If we have differences with people its ok, because this is the premise that we are all different, but to have differences rooted in fear it's not ok. Only when you see someone clearly taken to doing harmful acts are we to allow fear to grip us...Never should we **not** even allow ourselves the opportunity to understand the differences before we remain rooted in those types of isolated thoughts about others.

This fear of the unknown has many branches, but one way it could be perceived is RISK. Taking risk, is it worth the risk, No...it's too risky... When thought about from this angle we can usually see procrastination develop because the person under goes a lot of stress when they try to contemplate any risks they are currently faced with. I have done many things in life, and held many titles from the peon on the totem pole to one of the highest, I have taken business risk, relocated so many times I have lost count, changed jobs also beyond count, and now I have taken on the role as an Educator/ an amateur author in my spare time...Writing this book is probably the largest risk I have ever undertaken in the my professional career. Without intent of bragging, it takes a lot of courage to put your thoughts into a concerted manner such as this, and then share it with everyone in the world. I really don't expect any riches or excessive fame, I mainly write because it provides me an artistic outlet for self-expression...I don't expect anyone I know to support me or my writing, although I offer to share. It's funny how the people closet to us won't listen to us, while people you cross paths with on some common ground will...They say the first one to come to visit you in the hospital is the most significant in loving/caring for you; I think that analogy applies to far broader issues. While people fail to take risk of their own, you will find jealousies toward those who take risk all the time. Out of the box thinkers, visionaries, artistic, dreamers...character that drives innovation & ideas; to create something in the mind and bring it out to the tangible world. There's no greater feeling! If I reach one reader in a profound way, I'm satisfied...Never do I nor have I depended on anyone's lips service; if I did then maybe It would affect my tenacity to create and or take risk. Instead I do what feels right in my heart, following that has never disappointed me, while faith in people always will.

But again, when a person chooses to put off things that affect their person then they are effectively hurting themselves. Oppressed not just by society, they have now begun to oppress themselves by not willing to deal with these issues of fear. Risk or fears of the Unknown when measured against solid research, self-assessment and faith should be enough to aid anyone in taking action. Unfortunately society offers way too many options of distraction and false assessments of ourselves. Hour after hour the commercials lest symptoms until we feel as though the commercial has our name written all over it, so we buy into the option of prescriptions instead of actually dealing with ourselves. Or we become followers of Dr. Phil, Dr. Oz or Oprah... People today have become fearful of each other's differences whatever they may be, but is this because we are actually afraid of ourselves. Are we so displaced and wrapped up in our own personal lies about ourselves that we fail to see the good in others? It takes one to know one...or the other quote we recognize in others what we recognize in ourselves...Differences seem to be the only things constantly debated, and put forth in society; while the option of displaying all that we share and have in common are ignored...How can anyone who isn't honest with themselves first be able to really have a genuine relationship with anyone. Honesty and integrity in the world today are fleeting characteristics in people. Few of us have genuine friendships that have with-stood the test of time and evils in the world today...Even in our own families, bonds have been destroyed from two income families & the desire of woman to work; City life leaving the 3 or 4 children families as memoires of the 1970's and beyond. The strong family bonds between siblings, cousins and even child with parent are today so easily affected by petty differences and cause families not to speak sometimes for years. What is the problem with everyone? Why can't we be happy for other people when we seem to be at the moment less fortunate; and when we are fortunate why we can't say kind words to those who are struggling? Why is everything money? Even when someone wants help, they don't want your words...they would much rather take the money. How is money going to help you deal with the realities about yourself? Wouldn't you rather learn how to fish instead of asking for a fish each day? Nobody is perfect and we all have our issues...

Speaking from myself now, I can honestly say that I have never feared the unknown, or uncertainty to the degree that it stopped me...Sure I have been uncomfortable at times but never fearful to the point of irrational ways of thought or control over myself. I don't say this to paint myself in brighter colors than anyone who is reading, I only mention it because I truly understand how this disease of irrational fear can take anyone out of reality...I know many people today from my childhood, young adult life as well as now that have always been controlled by fear. Fear has robbed them of any and all of their dreams; their ambitions are now nothing more than words that have been rehearsed now more than anything else they have said. It's the same song and dance...Every time I return home, or see someone in this condition it first hurts my heart because often times I have tried to encourage these people. Looking in from the outside we can sometimes offer good words of encouragement to help seeing in them what they themselves don't. But you can only say so much. Stuck in time, their lives captured in the last good moment; instead of moving on they try to relive that last good moment over & over...You will find people in the same place, wearing similar clothing, doing the same actions, speaking the same words as if time has literally stood still. That is because for them it has! They are stuck in the mind, and although the mind is very delicate its power is immense. We have our physical existences through the mind, and the heart...So when the mind is capture so is the body. The world is constantly changing but to this person it doesn't change at all. They still see the world as it last appeared to them when they had a life not controlled by fear. Prior to the fear they may have been normal, but afterwards you see a drastic change in them because your reference once shared with them begins to widen, especially if your life is moving forward. Changes for them are relevant to that of the world they are stuck in: whatever the influence is the release of new music, parties, sneakers/clothing, cars and the likes...they don't see changes in the economy, or the world because these things don't matter to them. I don't understand really, but I guess I never could. My Mother, I thank Allah for her and ask for the creators mercy on her soul Ameen; instilled in me at a very young age a hard work ethic. That work ethic still lives within me today...Then not understanding the reasons for so much hard work around our house, I complained to her at times for it...but then as I started to understand more it made sense. Besides that all the neighbors would constantly compliment us on how well kept our yard was.

When my parents first bought the house it need a lot of work, the lot was normal, and there was a 50ft ditch to the south of the house that extended to the corner. It had large trees & bushes of all sorts...My father bought it had it cleared and filled it in. We planted grass and within a couple seasons you never would know the ditch was there prior. Never did I work without her talking to me...She was a hard worker herself, but as I would dig huge holes for her yard trees to be planted many of them 3feet deep or more, she would be giving me an ear full of advice and wise words or true stories of her own life. Many of these words would be words my grandfather or grandmother told her. Working and listening and then pondering over all that she said. I really understood her, what she was saying and what she was warning me about. In life there is absolutely NO need to be fearful to the point that your entire life is taken from you. There is no reason for you to go through life not expecting to get knocked down HARD...you will just need to pick yourself up and keep going. If you wait too long to try again it will be harder for you. Like the rider of a horse who takes a nasty spill off the horse, if he/she doesn't get right back on and continue that fear of being thrown off again may prevent him/her from ever riding again. Life is really no different. I come to tears thinking about anything regarding my Mother...but really instilling in our children these lessons you really only have one opportunity to do so. If you leave this too long and allow other bad influences to become rooted in them then your battle will be twice as hard. Like any sickness, you will now need to rid them of the sickness before you are able to make them strong again. Bitter divorces and breakups are robbing children of fatherly advice, and absentee parents are allowing societal influence to teach their children. It pains my heart to have been a victim of this myself...Wanting to do all that I mention to you now, but young women often act in spiteful ways in divorces/breakups and they use the children to try to hurt the fathers...No one suffers more than the children. Distance makes it worse, and their not knowing or understanding compounded with time is a recipe for a major bomb. This is why many of the youth are angry, carry chips on their shoulders, and live life in a not caring manner. Whatever, I don't care their favorite words...My advice to all mothers out there, don't use your children against their fathers! Secondly, understand that the world is a huge obstacle in overcoming for many of the men out there who are truly trying to be a part of the children's lives. What they can't offer in ways of material goods doesn't devalue the PRICELESS advice a good father can give...The re-establishment of roles between men & women is something that needs to be implemented because society is today upside down on this topic. A lot of women are WAY out of line, and there are a lot of men who aren't acting the part...

All the comforts we grow accustomed to are another set of conditions that when threatened in any way will trigger the emotion of fear. The current crises in the West financial system and of the resulting economies, civil unrest across Europe and lack of jobs in America has forced many into the fear of the unknown without choice. So, how is it when forced to deal with something we do so of course by no will of our own, but never choose to do so willing prior to not having a choice? Excessive, affluent lifestyle is another mechanism that will cause extreme fear and denial of reality by those affected by it. Look at the rise of suicide in the Western World; an estimated 1 million people worldwide take their lives by suicide every year. It is estimated that global annual suicide fatalities could rise to 1.5 million by 2020. Worldwide, suicide ranks among the three leading causes of death among those aged 15–44 years. Suicide attempts are up to 20 times more frequent than completed suicides. The fear of dealing with ourselves, and usually forced to face society in a manner that is not acceptable to us ultimately causes many people to take their own lives...Living life trying to keep up with the "Jones" as we say, causes huge amounts of stress in keeping pace and when the humiliation of losing in this race comes it causes so many people to take their lives rather than appear as they are. In 2003, in the United States, whites and Asians were nearly 2.5 times more likely to kill themselves than were blacks. What could be more supporting to what I have just said? The lower rung of economic/financial status has been a motive for people to strive hard to gain material wealth, but when the threat of losing it all comes they are not able to deal with the new realities. Lower income races of people actually have a blessing in the struggles that they face in that they are more so rooted in true reality and not aloft in some unsustainable bubble that one day will burst.

CHANGE

For better or worse quite like the vows between the bride and groom; the promise of change is inevitable: for richer or poorer, sickness & health until death bids us apart...Change is inevitable so resistance to it is really quite worthless. All things in this life are designed with the opposite condition. I guess in order to appreciate happiness you need to have experienced periods of sadness, or times of struggle with times where struggle is eased a bit to enjoy. This up & down is the roller-coaster of life and because human beings are prone to forgetfulness & ingratitude we are subjected to this perpetual cycle of being take up and down in order to constantly reprove us...But many people don't want to accept this condition of life and try to live life on the highest, linear line they can achieve. Sustaining this condition at any cost this includes human life. In denial that this life is not sustainable and not able to deal with the least bit of stress, the masses of people buy into the idea that money will rid them of the lowly stresses they experience at lower income brackets. We miss the point all together and never do we consider the lives of people who seem to have it all. We're completely sold on the notion that we will have that linear line that represents smooth sailing upon life until we leave this world. But with more comes more responsibility and problems. Change being the constant in the equation of life, we should learn that we can never alter it or cancel it out...like that of PI=3.14 change is something we are stuck with. On a more positive sounding note, change often brings a renewal to that in which is being changed i.e. the earth in it seasons and or the changes we experience within our own person. Unlike the seasons, wither we have brought about this change ourselves from some sort of decision or by its own design; change has many hidden rewards that would have never been regarded if we had the option to resist otherwise. Thus is the purpose for change by its own design; knowing that mankind can be so stubborn or defiant towards change, we sometimes undergo change whither we like it or not. In fact, I would retract that statement to say that change brought about without our consent is more than the change we agree too. Reason I say this is obvious as we are not here writing our own scripts in the Broadway Play called life... it is the other way around. Everything about our bodies is changing moment by moment. Not one of us can alter the script that is already written for us, for the creation towards fulfilling its purpose of being created in the first place. Therefore if we learn to see everything in this way with an attitude of acceptance, we will be more aware of the good that comes with change. Whether that change is apparently good, or appears to be bad; we will still be enabled to take the good from the good and also from that which appears to be bad. One thing that comes to mind when I think about this point just made is the psyche of people. Dynamic in every way down to the uniqueness of our fingertips...but something we seem to share is a settled type of attitude upon the condition we are in. Be it lofty or lowly people have a chronic disposition when settled to long. Bad character, mannerisms, competitiveness for material things, jealousies, envies etc...Like an icebreaker; change comes to break up all that cold heartedness. I mention on the negative mannerism because in my opinion it's more relevant since people who accept change and go with it. People who try to induce change themselves as well as accept that change that is inevitable you find them to have more humble ways & positive demeanor. It makes since too if you consider a living example of a person where change is upon them, but they still stubbornly try to refuse. They refuse and refuse thinking they will overcome, but always they will find themselves the losers. Our arms are too short to box with Allah/God, to even attempt to do so is quite foolish. Much like the brat kid you see in the market with is mother when she tells him/her to put back whatever it is they have taken off the shelf and put into the cart. They don't listen & ignore her as she continues to shop...maybe thinking she will forget it's there and they will get there way in the matter. But she reaches in overpowering them physically, authoritatively, and financially. We are powerless in the world around us, even the richest people are reminded of their mortal weaknesses with illness, misfortune & death...My mother use to tell, "Me sometimes you will need to flush the toilet on life" LOL...What this means is when life begins to stink bad you need to flush...Or when you come to realize that the people around you are nothing more that leaches or sharks flush...wasteful matter is bloating it's sickening so we need to make sure we all stay as regular as possible in keeping ourselves free from constipation in the literal and metaphorical sense.

In a world of finite resources how is it that the "American Dream" model is package and sold as something good & really achievable by all who try? Because you have to be a sleep in order to have the dream, Best said by late comedian George Carlin. Yes, disconnected with the truth about reality. Unfortunately the world we live in isn't interested in this linear line being achieved by everyone. Why? Well ask yourself if the entire world lived in a state of affluence we would rape the earth dry from consumption, and who would be left to serve everyone? Yes, I think in a fair society governed on just principles, and not given into greed; life would be manageable upon a state of no stress and less fear upon people in consideration to their achievements, uncertainties, livelihoods and differences. But the capitalist, Western model is setup to be the society who is served while others play the role of servant. This paints the "Mona Lisa" for today's condition and struggle that is upon the West to stay above water; while the East is experiencing a revival of markets, development & ideals. What's crazy is the West has basked in the exploitation of others for the past century speaking only from the American Era...And leaving the impression upon everyone benefiting from this, that what had been achieved was going to last forever. What the West has experienced was the setting up and culmination of systems already exploited by Empires prior to her own existence at the top. Now that change is imminent and the media is again at work painting the evil picture of images along with the rhetoric and newly invented words for the age to induce fear upon the notion of "Change"... Society is being encouraged by every facet of media there is towards resisting change by any means...But the very slogan of President Obama was "Change, YES WE CAN". Tell me how can America sustain what it has today? It's currently so mired in debt that economically/financial it's impossible to recover from; she no longer is a leader in innovation, manufacturing, engineering, sciences etc... The only thing America has is her military. Having said that, the military industrial complex has been the driving force behind the American economy for the past 20yrs for sure; while some may argue further back than that. The fascist, imperialistic option she is exercising today is the rejuvenation based on others wealth, a sustenance she has grown to depend upon. While the elite class begs to maintain their wealth (pending collapse of the $) by turning the other cheek in military occupation in oil rich Muslim countries, and influence to absorb Eastern countries into the control of the U.N.; it is the sole source of maintaining world reserve currency status...Driven by her Machiavellian type tactics she would rather be feared than loved by other governments as fear last longer; while on the other side of the coin she employs her popular celebrity to the masses of people towards love. Now that the world has come to this critical junction in history it is now upon the people of the world as well as our respective governments to make critical decisions. The people of America are also being called upon to make choices that will definitely impact the world. Moral choices are also now at the forefront of these decisions since many jobs are solely for the perpetuation of her current path. No more is having a job a good excuse because of the conditions that your job many help to sustain...We have to begin to hold everyone responsible for his or her actions & roles in society. Think about it!!! What have people been doing for the past 50 plus years? Trying to buy into obtaining that linear line of success to ride high...well it's not the reality and now the inclination to go off to college obtain a degree in something doesn't guarantee that linear line anymore, but definitely will secure you in debt. People have left the simpler means of living and have all followed suit in trying to do what others have done in acquiring more and more until you acquire so much you become a slave to it in maintaining it. This is now why you can't leave the job you have today that plays a significant role in killing, exploiting, corrupting, and undermining the world. Morally, you may want to leave, but you are fearful of what is to become of you & your family if you resign etc. This is definitely not a good place to be in, and for anyone who is still free to make choices, I suggest you decide always towards that in which will keep you with choice.

Since the second war with Iraq, in which Saddam Hussein was actually captured and taken out of power, people working in the intelligence communities have one after another been plagued by their consciousness to not just walk away from that in which they were a part of, but they have also blown the whistle illuminating the details of their operations from within. This type of action takes huge **cohonizes** as our Spanish comrades might say...I applaud their efforts as a citizen of the world; because this should be the most common base thing each and every one of us shares. We are all trapped here in this world until death takes us away from here, so differences shouldn't be a factor in the face of clear and present danger...On the federal level we see this whistle blowing taking place but what about on the local levels of government? Have there been any courageous people to lead the way for consciousness to overcome the choices you have in choosing professions? Really people I think this should be considered very seriously...If you had someone standing on the corner of the neighborhood you lived in or hanging out at the school your children attended selling them drugs you would want to see this person arrested. So what is the difference in working in a position that does the same sorts of illegal practice? There are professions within the professional spectrum that are just as illegal if not more so and instead of jail people take their salaries, live in the sub-burbs and take their kids to soccer every weekend... Go figure! Have we the people been completely flipped upside down and left that way? Or are the hearts of the people now inside out, so that we now take what is wrong to be correct and what is correct to be wrong? I think so...what else could it be? The people have given the Multi-National Corporations completely everything in controlling them by chasing the material world they have marketed and advertised to us so we run out and buy things we absolutely don't need. In doing so, we have become slaves to those same immoral jobs we may have, or maybe it's the boss whom you know makes very shady business deals...whatever the case maybe the people have to change. Take back your independence and control over your own life by ridding

yourself of any and all debt. Reduce your spending to only buying that in which you need and will sustain you, stop trying to stay in fashion, and learn more ways to be resourceful on your own. Plant gardens in the backyard or anywhere you have space. Rooftop gardens like that of my own do very

well...they are exposed to rain water and sunlight whenever these conditions are present and they give you the best feeling in the world after they have begun to grow. Picking from the garden vegetables to

add to dishes prepared in the home is an unbelievable joy. I really don't want to sound like someone's life coach here but it's crazy how people have gotten out of touch with these simple things, many of which will bring pleasure in maintaining. Prone to stress a garden will help you with that. Try also riding your bicycle to work, wake early enough to have a coffee and bagel, crossiant, donut... whatever is your pleasure and head off to work on the bicycle giving yourself enough time that you don't need to rush, but instead enjoy the ride. I sometimes stop at a little place nearby one location I teach at before my time and relax to have a proper breakfast before I go in. When we learn to take change in stride you will then be able to take from the best of that change...but if you are the type to always being resistant then those changes may overwhelm you. I think that people often associate freedom to that only of physical bondage; but true freedom is complete independence like that of a farmer.

Owning your land, digging a well, having livestock for milk & meat, poultry with the eggs they also provide, and of course the garden. This type of person is his/her life is seldom interrupted by fluctuations in the economy etc. Sure there may be years when crop doesn't grow well, or weather happens etc. but that's life...but theses man-made changes happening all over aren't resistive to

you and I if we are dependent on society for our meal tickets. Even the business owner is dependent on his customers having work so they will have money to spend with him. We don't need to have huge 12 person farmers, but anything that frees you from something is little by little making you freer. Selling the glitz and glamour of the city life instead of land ownership in the countryside is one way they have fooled all of us into becoming enslaved...forever entangled in the web or working for someone that includes the business owner. Your livelihood still depends on your customer. Don't want to do it yourself, here buy this; don't want to wait any longer buy this; The decisions we have made and the choices we will make should always be in line with changing or choosing for the better. The world around us isn't going to get better if we ourselves are incapable of doing so. Negligence imparted by selfish living, a culture of greed/credit, fast food application of doing & wanting in a rush...no longer patient, the drive through has changed the pace of the world.

Death

Self-explanatory to say the least...how many people are afraid or in fear of death? Almost everyone would say I am if asked this question. So, let's talk more so about why are people fearful of this although they know it is the most sure thing in existence that one day we will all have to die. It's really quite simple really...people who are the least prepared for death are those most attached to the current life!!! They see this life as one life to live, make the best of it and so they live without bounds and live never contemplating death at all. In fact it's that phobic type of fear spoken about in previous chapter; they avoid at all cost this type of fear...Anything that reminds them of death they avoid it. I know of people who will not even go to the funerals of their loved ones to avoid the contemplation of death. Remember everything has its opposite, and the opposite of life is death. We can never enjoy fully life without the contemplation of death. As most people see thinking about death as something bad and never could it bring any type of happiness in thinking about it. But I beg to differ, if you truly understand the purpose of life you will find that your life will begin to take on new meaning and purpose. Nobody is Immortal, but think of yourself living along side of someone who was immortal; while you yourself were mortal. What do you think the differences between you would be? Don't think too hard about this question. Keep it simple. The one who is immortal would be more than likely to take much more about his life for granite than the one who is mortal. You see knowing that you have to die one day, should bring a more complete fullness to your life making it more enjoyable and precious to you. But this is NOT the case...We take absolutely everything and everyone for granite. We don't even count the countless blessings that we do have. If in your next doctor visit the doctor told you; you didn't have much time left, less than a year...How would you feel? What would you do? I'll tell you...Immediately you would have a humbling feeling overtake you that reminds you that you are not so special, you're not immortal, remind you of your arrogance, of all the things you have done wrong, and less about what you have done correctly. Why? Do you see all this consideration of ME, ME, ME first? Of course, because no one else is willing to take your place; when you go you have to go alone. Nothing of this world is going to come to your aide, and nothing of this world is going to delay it from happening. Who knows how long this self-reflection will last, I guess that depends on how you have lived...then if not overwhelmed with wrong living and taken by depression you will then think about family and friends. Then you might think about everything you've done in life and more so what you haven't done. Maybe if you had the means to do some of the things you intended or wanted to do you might try doing that. Ironic how the news of death wakes a person up, but while they still have life they allow the television to keep them in a state of sleep chasing the DREAM!

Death the destroyer of desires & pleasure...you should always contemplate it. Now in thinking about it you don't have to think about the gross details, however you shouldn't sugar coat it so much that it becomes something that isn't realistic. I can remember my first real contemplation of death that may come as a surprise to most people who know something of the journey of my life. Anyway, the first time I thought about death was after I watched a movie that I can no longer remember the title too. The story line was about a young boy who was a track star at his school, long distance running, and later was diagnosed with cancer after collapsing during one of his bouts. I was maybe 12 or 13yrs. Old at the time but I was so taking in by the story line that it scared me to death. I had nightmares for maybe 3months; I'm still able to recall how spooked I was. Then I didn't understand many things I do today, and that explains the reason why I was so scared. No different to anyone today despite age, if you live solely to eat, sleep & crapt then death probably scares the hell out of you. My first personal experience with death I was 18yrs old and seated on a plane with my rifle between my legs in full military gear...I hadn't been out of high school a year, and now aboard a 18hr flight to the middle-East I thought about a lot things. The first thing that come to mind was all the war movies I had seen; *Saving private Ryan*, *Full Metal Jacket* my favorite with the funny Drill Sargent and the jelly donut scene; *Apocalypse Now,* and the likes... I tried picturing myself in any of the scenarios in those movies and asking myself, "what will you do if..."? Over and Over until sleep over took me. When I woke, I still had several hours left in the flight, and after my senses returned to me making me aware to the fact that I wasn't in my own bed, I returned to the contemplation of death in war. The one thing that helped me not just in these thoughts but throughout my entire time in the theater of war was my faith. My mother deeply religious taught us many things, and like other times she would talk to me she spoke to me prior to my departure over the phone because I was stationed elsewhere. She told me she was so proud of me first, and no what happened remember to take care of myself, don't do anything stupid. She knew about some of the elderly friends I had and asked me, "Which of them had the most common sense"? I told her Sgt. Ball so she told me, "Then you stay close to him". LoL...Yeah she was funny too...So, I checked my faith during that flight. I mean, I CHECKED MY FAITH ON THAT FLIGHT...I asked the creator to protect me, allow me to return in one piece not broken up missing limbs; BUT if I am to die here to except me!!! I swear to you these were my words and what I came to terms with. I would later doze off again a few more times but as the flight time narrowed to arrival I couldn't sleep. Nervousness came in to me. Like the nervousness before a basketball game in front of a crowd. I want to perform well but only after beginning do you find a sense of calm. I wasn't afraid, instead I felt more anxiety. When we got in country, I was completely at peace with myself and accepted whatever my fate was to be. I remained this way the entire time. Then One night on a trip back to the South of Saudi Arabia where we had left some supplies; while loading the trucks (only 6 of us on this trip) I was standing look out while the others where in a chain like passing what was to be loaded from the connex to the truck quickly. I saw a red streak cross the sky, and then I saw a bunch more. Then maybe 15seconds later we all began to hear the explosions. The others had no Idea of what was happening, I was the only one who saw the patriot missiles launch out to intercept the incoming scud missiles. I immediately alarmed everyone "GAS, GAS, GAS"...Everyone puts their gas mask on, then rushing back to our respective vehicles to get our gas suits and put them on. We practiced this exercise over and over putting on the mask and suit, but now it was for real. I would much rather catch a bullet than be poisoned I thought; inhaling some poisonous, toxic whatever and left to die a slow, agenizing death...After we were all in our suits we locked up the connex strapped down the equipment and headed out. We began to drive back to the city area still seeing more red streaks cross the sky...then as we traveled down the main road in a seemingly ghost town due to all the overhead missiles. One gets by the patriot defenses and hits a building to my left with such force it's unreal. It's close to mid-night, the temperature is still nearly 100° F and after seeing the missile hit this building a city block to our front and to the left...I swerve and fight to control the vehicle from the impact and I immediately begin to sweat like I had never sweat before in my life. So much so, that it quickly added to the sweat already gathering in my air-tight mask; the level in my mask covered my mouth and was coming close to nose level. The mask, while wearing it distorts your depth perception, so if walking it appears as if you have no legs and you are walking on your chin...the same when you are driving. I was now fearful, but not taken to irrational panic. When we got to the military garrison in the city maybe 15mins later I had begun to gurgle in my mask...the built in hose for the mask made to punch into the top of our canteens to drink water without exposure if ever in a situation such as this, is only made to suck in, so it won't work as a drain...This perfected design doesn't offer me any relief, but thank God the all clear sign was given after testing the air quality with special devices and I quickly lifted the mask from my chin and all the sweat came gushing forth. My body was soaked as well under the suit. I had my regular full fatigues and boots on, and now this charcoal lined chemical suit in 100°F weather. It was as if I had jumped into a swimming pool with my clothes on. Few more situation occurred but that's another story...I mention this one because It was one of the most complex of dealing with the outside threat of missiles and the inside threat of drowning in my own mask...I don't know how I have been able to overcome many situations that I have faced, but I tell you sincerely that no matter the danger I accept the fate that is upon me. To fight with that would surely cause panic and panic isn't something that benefits a situation it only cause the situation to be worse.

In Essence to ignore death is really the misunderstanding about life...Death comes before life! What do I mean? Before you & me are alive in this world we were dead non-existent...from death you were given life. From life we are returned to death yet again only to be given life again but the next life will be eternal. Yes, I know some of you don't believe that and that's your prerogative; but for those of you who do believe in resurrection, day of reckoning/accountability then this is the truth. It is the truth even if you don't believe...Another supporting factor to this point of death before life is the cycle of day and night. The Night precedes the day, not the other way around like most people have been taught. The Gregorian calendar is the pagan calendar and for the most part the newest type of calendar used; but the lunar calendar dates back to antiquity. The night begins just after sunset, while the day begins just after sunrise. For example: on Friday after sunset Saturday (Yawm-ul-Sabd or Day of Sabbath) begins, and the Saturday day begins after sunrise. Sunday (Yawm-ul-ahad or 1st Day) begins Saturday after sunset...Even if you were to contemplate the creation story of creation; space is a vast darkness before the creation. Genesis says the Earth was dark a void, and the word of God moved upon the earth he said, "Let there be light", and there was light...But this statement is completely not true both literally and scientifically. Why? Because back in the days when people still thought the earth was flat etc. they also thought the earth was the center of creation, which everything revolved around the earth...well come to find out that the earth isn't flat nor does anything but the moon revolve around her. That being the case we know that the creation of the Sun was created first given light to a dark universe, and then the creation of the planets that orbit etc... So even on a scientific level the bible is not in agreement, but that's another time, another book God willing...

My mother used to wake up really early in the morning, before dawn (what we Muslims call the time just before Fajr), and she would make her coffee & sit at the table looking out of this huge picture window that over looked the countryside. I would travel up most Friday afternoons or evenings after work if I wasn't away to spend the night with her and my step-father Charlie. We would make bomb-fires and roast some meat, marshmallows and just hang-out and talk around the fire way into the night. I remember we made one fire out of some old wooden yard furniture that was made out of trees we had cut down in the yard from our childhood home...these chairs were as old as I was almost and extremely weathered. Snow, rain, summer sun year after year...Now they were really dry rotten, so we tossed them in the pit along with some other wood, stick and anything else we needed to burn for garbage etc. My brother Aaron squirts almost a whole can a lighter fluid onto the heap and so when the match was thrown in the Fire JUMPED UP!!! Immediately it was a roaring fire...We all fell back on our butts and panicked due to the size of the Fire. We were probably 50yrds from the house so there was no danger of the house or anything catching fire...the problem was that the fire was so big you could probably see it from space. In the pitch black countryside, it lit up everything. The garden hose wouldn't reach the fire, so we stretched it as far as it would go, and made a water bucket assembly line trying to doss the fire to a more humble flame. After all no one could sit next to this fire it was WAY TO HOT! Anyway we laughed about that for months after, as I laugh now in remembering it. But no matter how late we would stay up, my mother would be up 4-4:30am each morning sitting in the window...Sometimes she would come and force me to get up too, and sit with her. On one occasion she asked me a profound question...She asked me, "Why do you think animals, mainly dogs/cats, die so young"?

Most of us know that dog/cat years are 7yrs for every 1yr to humans in order to see their years in a human reference...but if taken in comparison of year for year with humans they live 7 times shorter lives. I didn't answer, just thought about why she was asking me this. We always had dogs growing up, German Schnauzers' and at this point and think it was Schnauzer #6 or 7; but it had been a long time since the last one passed on and Maggie the current one was sitting at my feet wanting me to play with her. I didn't answer for a long time maybe 3 mins. My mother when she asked the question she wasn't even looking at me, she was still gazing out the window. I guess I was trying to figure out the reason for then such a strange question as it might relate to something she's trying to say to me about herself. I finally gave her that shrug of the shoulders and early morning, "I don't know". She took my reply without notion, still staring out the window. She lifted up cup, took a sip of coffee and after she put the cup back on the table she turned to me and said, "Maybe it's because they have learned how to love unconditionally". I didn't get it right then, but I was trying...so she went on to explain the thought after the statement..."have you ever noticed how dogs no matter what love you? I mean when you leave go away, miss feeding them, or make them wait to let them out in the morning, or spend time with them outside etc., they will still love you". "Every time they see you it's as if they are seeing you for the first time". "Anything that has that much love in them doesn't need to be confined in this world that lacks love, so maybe this is their pass to leave sooner than us". She explained things to me in such a way I would think about what she said for A LONG TIME and remember with clarity as I now share it with you. Even when I was little this is how she spoke to me in our moments, she knew how to reach me with words that were so full of wisdom...Deep thought, self-reflection, self-correction towards something constantly better if you don't have this you are already dead!!! So many people today are lifeless, they draw breathe have a pulse, but they are dead...the walking dead! It is only in the throes of death do they wake up and give thought to something more than themselves. You are not living if you don't have this type of reflection about yourself first. To live the best life you can ever imagine is to carry out every deed of your day as if it is your last. When and if you reach this level of awareness then you will finally arrive to a point in life unimaginably beautiful, full of joy in the times of struggle, confident in the face of defeat, vibrant to others around you, and a high on life that is unsurpassed...No worldly gain can give you this sort of felicity, not money, not your spouse, not your children nothing...you have to reach this on your own. Each of us is the owner of our own death & life...these two things have to be figured out and carried out by the individual; no one can help you. When you reach your high then you can teach others how to get there i.e. your children but if you don't then you can't, nor should you expect to be carried up by someone else. You have to work for this ALL ON YOUR OWN. Make the best of your time, for that time is constantly ticking toward the day in which you try to hide from, but no matter where you are it will find you. In your penthouse atop the tallest building, beneath the sea, at work, at home, in good, in bad, in laughter, in pain, youth, or old no matter what you are doing or where you are...remember to be sure about that in which you do, in that in which you support, in that in which you call too, in that in which you believe because when Malikul Mawt (Angel of Death) comes and tells you to give up your soul you want to be prepared and in a place within yourself constantly that you are prepared to depart. Like a planned tripped, you may pack a few days before; this is THE trip everyone should be packed for ahead of time...So this reminder of one day, be it right at this moment, sometime today, tomorrow, this week, next week, this month, next month, this year, next year...or the next 50yrs you and I will experience this inevitable event, so you should do you best at making yourself ready for that day.

Xenophobia

In the previous chapters I have basically spoken about fear from observation, personal experience, and of the little I have studied in regards to human nature in psychiatry classes and books. But now on a much larger scale let's look again to the world stage and see how the culture of the world stage and its fear has changed over the years. Going back 100 years from the current year of 2014 brings us to the year of 1914, which just by fluke am I able to bring to the attention this most ironic consideration of fear then happening on the world stage...the date is June 28, 1914 and gun shots have just taken the life of Archduke Francis Ferdinand heir to the throne in Austria-Hungary. The country mourning and gripped by the desire of justice, One month later on July 28, 1914 Austria-Hungary declares war on Serbia beginning the "Big War" as is was earlier called, known today as World War 1. Earlier on, Russian political maneuvering and spreading the influence of communism, the region now was destabilized in the peace accords, which were already fracturing in what was known as "the powder keg of Europe". In 1912 and 1913, the First Balkan War was fought between the Balkan League which includes Greece, Bulgaria, Serbia and Montenegro; directed at the already fracturing Ottoman Empire. The resulting Treaty of London further shrank the Ottoman Empire, creating an independent Albanian State while enlarging the territorial holdings of Bulgaria, Serbia, Montenegro, and Greece. The World Powers of Britain, Germany, Austria-Hungary, Russia & Italy proposed terms to the Ottoman Empire:

- To release all European territory west of Enos on the Aegean Sea and Midia on the Black Sea and give it to the Balkan league.

After the series of wars in the Balkans and then finally the assassination already mentioned the world then was plunged into the First World War...The trigger was the assassination and you will find that a trigger has always existed in many of the world's conflicts to seemingly undermine any diplomacy underway or in the works. In brief by the end of the war, four major imperial powers—the German, Russian, Austro-Hungarian and Ottoman empires—ceased to exist. The influence of the world was now open to opportunity again...The map of Europe was redrawn, with several independent nations restored or created. The League of Nations formed with the aim of preventing any repetition of such an appalling conflict. It was the first international organization whose principal mission was to maintain world peace. Its primary goals, as stated in its Covenant, included preventing wars through collective security and disarmament, and settling international disputes through negotiation and arbitration; Other issues in this and related treaties included labor conditions, just treatment of native inhabitants, human and drug trafficking, arms trade, global health, prisoners of war, and protection of minorities in Europe. At its greatest extent from 28 September 1934 to 23 February 1935, it had 58 members. Incapable of preventing aggression by the Axis powers in the 1930s. Germany withdrew from the League with a renewed European nationalism and the German feeling of humiliation that contributed to the rise of fascism setting the conditions for World War II. Other countries would follow: Japan, Italy, Spain, and others. The onset of the Second World War showed that the League had failed its primary purpose, which was to prevent any future world war. The League lasted for 27 years its successor the United Nations (UN) replaced it after the end of the Second World War.

We now that America would also join in the War in 1917, but prior to her entry into the war President Woodrow Wilson on 19 August 1914 addressed congress with his public U.S. policy of "Neutrality"...It warned citizens against taking sides in the war out of fear of endangering the WIDER U.S. policy...Since the Caucasian people primarily had migrated to America from the countries that were now in conflict, so he was trying to promote the way of thinking towards neutrality based on the new foundation of America. He encouraged all public conversation in magazines, newspapers, barbershops and even the ministers to their congregations to take the stance of neutrality and keep an atmosphere of calm. The people of the United States are drawn from many nations and the sympathies of the people will vary accordingly. Anyone guilty of inciting or playing on the emotions of the people would be responsible for dividing the people into hostile camps of opinion, which in the least if not taken to actions would have profound affects to the unity of the country. These types of divisions would be fatal to the peace of mind and to the overall landscape of America...ethnic & individual duties taken a turn toward self-loyalties and not of the collective loyalty of the country. He closes along the lines of impartial thought & action, curbed sentiments to consider the whole and not take one party over another....

A far cry in comparison to today; Americans today are from all the lands of conflict currently held in aggression...Wow...the speech and actions in America don't resemble that from 100yrs ago. One word comes to mind when I ponder over what was done then verses now...Xenophobia! This type of fear has so many variations and typically comes about from relations and perceptions of an in-group (normal) towards that of an out-group (strange). Fear of losing identity, suspicion, aggression, and elimination of something for preservation of something else either based on truth or for a continuance of something already practiced. Xenophobia can also be seen from the angle of extraordinary exaltation of one culture over another. Again one being normal while the other(s) are seen as abnormal...Most governments are urged to take strong actions against manifestations of racism, or related intolerance that includes legislation and penal measures. Note my choice of the word "MOST" because we know when it comes to the United States of America she hasn't conformed to the encouragement of just legislation and or penal measures when dealing with her diverse citizenry. Why? The most obvious answer would be the perception of what group is considered and group(s) are not considered to be the normal population or citizenry. Often this is easily applied to that of immigrants as is often the case with fleeing Mexicans to America illegally. But since America is a land of immigrants this application applies to all those not in the ruling race or the race upon which the new State of America was founded. Subject citizens and others illegally entering are therefore seen as the group abnormal to the whole. Likewise, the languages and cultures that they bring as well... Cultured considered abnormity is the 2nd condition in which xenophobia can be built. In extreme cases societies can refuse entirely any opposing type of culture(s) besides that of itself...So; the policies of neutrality of 100yrs ago were for the eradication & prevention of this type of fear amongst the European descendant population that was now in America. Born out of colonialism xenophobia then was seen as normal by its practitioners', then adopted into the early formation of the New World, it has been the defining arrangement amongst the inhabitants of these new lands. Never really has any other type of idea or equality been transparently accepted. The civil war taking place to again prevent the division of the New country, and sold to the subjects as freedom to encourage their loyalty to the North to defeating the then very strong economical/financial South. But how can a country who drafts and implements into the founding fabricate a document that would hold anyone not free (being enslaved) as 3/5 a human being ever become a country free of xenophobia towards something it holds and see as different? The old sentiments have been passed down year after year, decade after decade, century after century...and still there is no clear sight of its complete eradication. This classical conditioning of seeing others not like unto yourself as alien you would think would find its place eventually under the basket with all other foolish practices of people throughout the years. True many old ways have loosened, and the interaction across racial lines has been seen now for the better part of 50yrs or so...but politically there is still a problem. Legislation and penal measures have long plagued Black communities and activities toward a more organized voice politically. At least some of us have heard about all the horror stories of illegally targeting blacks in traffic stops without probable cause, falsified jailing of black suspects, and with the advent of cocaine in American cities the enormous increase of time with sellers of crack cocaine vs. powder cocaine…Because blacks are more than like to be sellers & or users

of crack cocaine due to it being cheaper than the powder source, more years of imprisonment where given.

Figure Igure I incarcerated Americans

The media has done, hands down the most efficient job at bringing fear to the main stream in America through cinema…Early movies like "**Gone with the Wind**", *The film has been criticized for its historical revisionism and glorification of slavery,* and the yet early purely racial depictions of blacks with oversized lips, song & dance seen as cheap entertainment, improper English speech, service attire etc. all played on the hearts towards further subjecting blacks in this way. By the 1970's it was the pimp, heroin pusher, gangster, criminal, big hat/fur coat, yellow Cadillac driver etc.

Assassinations' or leaders, infiltrations of organizations all done to undermine groups from the inside out, and plant seeds that for decades now have only harvested fruit of distrust between the people, corruption & hate within those whom eat from these trees. No longer visible this deep seated xenophobia has gone undergrown to sow its seeds of division. In need of a lower class to be in service to those in higher rungs of society but at the same time harboring such a profound hatred that you exercise all sorts of evils to kill and destroy an entire nation of people. Ethnocentrism and the false ideas of Eugenics married to the philosophy of Darwin's "**Therory of Evolution**", are all ways of seeking validity to the up kept madness. The ignorance of racism, and that of its bigger cousin nationalism is all rooted in evil and division; and one is no better than the other. Only in the last 20yrs have you seen blacks in Hollywood taking on new roles, but even with the advancement of roles they play we have to understand the change in the world's philosophy and the shift of xenophobia towards a new outgroup that isn't solely racial anymore but now more so directed at culture, with an emphasis on religion... now around the world through all of the open channels of reaching people. Media meaning television, radio, internet, publication, advertisement, law, and even the use of religion have now a new target to isolate & eradicate in the light of this new blend of world conspiracy seen as abnormal when in fact the practices and systems that are now failing are the abnormalities... History has shown us all the different models of governance:

1. The rule of Allah/Gods law over all things in the world (*By the Prophet, or Prophet/King with the likes of David & Solomon A.S. and Muhammad s.a.w.*)

2. The Caliphate (*Non-prophet, who enforces the laws of the creator*)

3. The King (*Man, who should rule with justice, and also rule according to Allah/Gods law...and if not knowledgeable in that law, then has a counsel that would advise him*)

4. Lastly, man-made systems (*communism, fascism, capitalism, & globalism*) Impossible to maintaining peace and justice for all, and they are almost always based on ethnocentrism, nationalism, xenophobia etc.

Fear of some level as been regulated when seen as a potential threat to the whole including the ruling class, but used to control subordinate groups with laws, penal measures, and even ministry in a type of calming doctrine towards acceptance to oppression while teaching a hope in prosperity through biblical verse interpretation.

There isn't any man-made system that is able to justly and fairly govern as we have seen the coming and going of these systems to date with globalism currently the economic system as the world prepares for the rule of Evil in the false form of Law. So, as the world and more relative to each of us our communities, cities and states literally come undone at the seams; confusion is at an all-time high. Sensing something is drastically wrong, I have listened to many people speak their fears & concerns. Fearful of tomorrow and what it might bring people are expressing that fear with isolation of themselves to non-physical interaction with the use of social media as a replacement to open, public conversation. People are afraid to speak out, and of being disassociated from the franchise of acceptance. So anyone with opinions or anything truthful to say is silenced due to fear of what the populace might say in reaction to their comments and or what the government may say. Even the youth are expressing themselves; this is what gives attitude and purpose to music of the day. Music Hip/hop, rock, punk, heavy metal often include lyrics of resistance & rebellion that speak directly to the confusion, frustrations, and fears of the young people. Not always gifted to the art of expression through speech, many easily ally with those who they identify with. Attitude has replaced kindness, and violence and replaced speech...Ignored in the pursuit of worldly gain the youth are now more than ever expressing that frustration through random acts of violence. The Columbine school shooting; Aurora, Colorado Theatre shooting; School shooting in Connecticut; countless other less memorable acts as well as the other acts of random violence taking place throughout America many of which are in broad daylight. The situation is no longer within a medicative realm and it now demands a more serious diagnosis besides the band aid type passiveness long given. Children are taken towards darkness in occult type beliefs of vampirisms, satanic rituals, and the dark dress of black clothing, lip stick, eye makeup, finger/toe nails, piercings of every kind. The guns & drugs of the ghettos are now finding their way into Middle America...and with it the influence of culture not like their own, often mimicking social groups of the black poor. The frustration is altogether more serious than many people choose to pay attention too; while those who benefit from the current ways of life ignore things altogether. It's always the rich or ruling classes that oppose the justice of change...They were the main opposition to all of the prophets of Allah in accepting their prophet hood & revelation, and they are still the opposers of revelation. I think the world in general needs to pay more seriousness attention to this last statement...Most of us not really religious in the least might see that statement in the light of stories of the past or folklore; not something you have really accepted as part of your faith. Considered more along the lines of some ancient story...it is in fact the premise of the conditions we face. Those who believe vs. those who don't...and life for those who don't is based on meaningless living driven to acquire and serve their own means. The problems of the world are disguised in the blatant disbelief of those who want the current conditions of the world, and that which is to come...Equality they don't want it...Justice they don't know it, peace they fight it and love they don't feel it.

Even when the world was governed in times of justice, peace, and love by other than our prophets, men of faith have been persuaded by worldly desires and thus planted seeds of corruption for change to also come in regards to those acts. Yes, change takes place on all levels reproving us to mistakes and deviance as well as to enlighten, reward & punish...In its absence people might learn the appreciation for what is best for them while being subjected to all the corruption of what they partook and allowed. We have to see the world in this way. Consequences to everything...It is time for people to start showing their faith and not just provide the lip service to proclaim what you identify with...but the exercise of that faith. What you differ with is an obligation of faith to rid yourself of that difference...pick up the book and read it; if you still don't understand or understand correctly get the appropriate explanation. Faith isn't biased, it doesn't harbor hate, or fear for the only fear we should all have is that towards living correctly in the eyes of the creator. If we can't do that, then this world will forever be at war...but the truth is what will endure and win in the end.

But in the arrogance of disbelief and still seeking to rule by division of the people of the world, the ritual of 911 happens which would bring about the mechanism to fight against the return to divine law uniting all people under the banner of One God, and Justice for all in the entire world...Unlike the allegiance to the united states of America and the republic for which it stands ONE NATION under God, indivisible, with liberty and justice for all...People of faith don't put country before Allah/God...The human family is far more important, and the diseases of xenophobia, ethnocentrism, nationalism etc. are all ingredients to that of disbelief. The well-being of one nation or one group while others are left to whatever condition befalls them is inhumane really, and it's an attitude not incorporated into any faith. So, why is it practice? Why is it followed? And why don't people understand that?

In her final stages of power and influence in the world, the American propaganda machine has shifted from that of its inner racism at least on the surface, while refocusing its efforts of fascist tactics of imperialist invasion into defenseless countries that will help with stimulating her own economy at home with the military industrial complex. Again feeding the deception of enemy culture, enemy or evil conspiracy towards her and her partners like Israel...when it is in fact the other way around; the attacker is seeking to play the victim while the victim is portrayed as the attacker. Defense against occupation, against corruption in implanted leaders who will carry out the wishes of those who put them into power, the temptations of capitalistic modernity for the agreement of allowing exploitation of resources in countries that still hold onto values or conservation both of humanity & of the earth. Islamic xenophobia throughout the world is used as the premise for occupation...100yrs ago as this chapter began the same conditions of xenophobia existed but with so many European monarchies all seeking the #1 spot, the battle ensued...however it was their influence to suck into the battle the Ottoman Empire that would bring down the already weakened world power upholding the banner of One God, and divine rule on earth. The jockeying of the smaller Eastern European powers & Russia for influence over the world would leave them all decimated in the aftermath leaving an Easy opportunity for Britain to emerge whom had all along played her hand in stirring the political bowl from the beginning. You will see Britain has played the role as instigator, two-faced renegor, & defector of politics throughout recent history dating back to her own rise and dealings in the crusades to the weakening of the Ottoman Empire. Today, we are again on the forefront of history...History is once again on the verge of repeating itself. The World has run through all the man-made systems of living absent Allah/God...communism came and went, fascism came and went, capitalism came and is currently failing meanwhile globalism is being implemented in the wake with the collapse and merging of currency & absorption in the United Nations of countries throughout the world. But only when the world is free of belief can it be a truly globally ruled society in the manner in which they seek...Mankind has nothing else to put in play besides the return of the rule of the creators law, so we see evil resisting until the end, but like any of your favorite movies the ending will be on the side of the good...

Mono-phobia

Most people can identify with a person(s) who act as a identifier for them personally. Usually we see this more with teenage groups as they seek to fit into different social groups in school etc. The Jock, the Preppies, the nerds, the geeks, the stoners, and the out-cast...groups teenagers find themselves trying to fit into for self-validation or recognition. But do these same groups exist for adults? Sure this exist in all of us...humans are social creatures and feel the need to share all the time. No one person is an island, meaning not one of us can go through life without speaking or sharing with anyone. You ever see the movie "**Castaway**" with Tom Hanks? After the plane crashes he finds himself the sole survivor on a deserted island. After some time goes by, I don't recall exactly, he begins to talk to the Wilson made volleyball. He puts it on a stand, and put some seed weed and other plant atop held on with a head band. Paints a mouth, eyes in a form of facial expression and he carries out full conversation with it; who knows maybe after sometime we might even begin to hear voices in response...The point being the human being is designed to share in life. In fact, it is the main purpose for marriage...Eve was created out of Adam's wish to have companionship! This innate desire was made part of man with the first of us and will always be until the last of us. We all have this desire...when our spouses are away we may feel a slight discomfort until they return, or when a close friend moves away, or when a child is made to stay with distant relatives or friends while you are away. All feel a discomfort until the norm is regained. You ever see yourself when you walk into a crowded waiting room? Say the room is full, but there is ample space to sit anywhere you would like; where do you think most people tend to sit? Yes, near to someone like themselves. Of course you see it the other way around as well, but it's an obvious eye soar because you can see the body language change immediately with that closeness of discomfort. Maybe a verbal hello or just a head gesture at best with a smirk as you take a seat. Hopefully the chair is positioned to give you a good view and didn't leave you staring at others in front of you who are also different. If it has left you this way, then hopefully you have a good book, games or ample people to text on your smartphone until you are called. Only then do you lift your head to scan the room...eye contact is usually avoided at all cost. We people are predictable, and your experience is likely that of my own, so why don't we get along and share in this understanding better? Our social group gravitational pull has never been stronger than it is today...the reason I say this is because yesterday people were inclined to gravitate in terms of race, culture or class; today people gather for the same but based on stronger sentiment and now also reinforced with political undertones. Even within groups that are together in one aspect but cross multiple lines of class, culture or language they will still be divided based on those differences. So well trained and programmed to only see the differences in people, the population is successfully divided upon everything under the sun. Add into the pot all the harbored jealousies, conditioned thoughts towards those different from yourself, and the overly aggressive manner of daily life and you have a very chaotic society. This nature of competitiveness is likened to the law of only the strong will survive, and thus people are hardened just to survive or in the least made to feel as though it is necessary. Are we human beings now being reduced to animals? We should really step back and take a look at ourselves...

At this very minute I have just concluded a conversation with my best friend Maurice. He always vents with me about his job, and the nature of the people in the workplace. Today, he told me about a supervisor he has who was also his supervisor on another job, but this guy has been out to get him. On the last job he was trying to create ways to have Maurice dismissed until he left to work for another company. He is now giving in passing the same dirty looks. What is it that makes people this way? Why are people ok with trying to take away the livelihood of others? Is hatred now exercised in a playful manner as though someone is playing the real life version of "Life or Monopoly"? He tells me now, he just goes to work hardly speaks to anyone, does his job and comes home. No more conversations at the lunch table, discussion over sports scores/events, or summer invites to home BBq's etc. The deception is now so bad that it is no longer worth the risk of sharing to much information about yourself with anyone, especially those you work with because jealousies seem to find their way back to your place of work. If seen as being in a position that is better than others it may cost you your job when the economy tightens and talks about whom to lay off start to bounce around. He goes on to say that now that he doesn't speak it seems to bring about more cutting of the eyes etc. I suggested to him that now maybe his lack of words is perceived in a fearful manner because no one knows his thoughts anymore...Speaking offers those around us some insight into what we are thinking, although it doesn't expose all thought, it at least tells everyone what is going on in the moment. Some people can't deal with silence in the least...it's like they are constantly running from their conscious, so silence is avoided. Constantly seeking ways of dialogue they are never without speaking until sleep over takes them. But there is a new phenomenon taking place...with the tightening of jobs, and the deep desire of material things and privilege has created the occupational spy and a new type of Uncle Tom. Like a woman who might sleep her way to the top, these people often of your own race and background are put in positions over those in whom they wish to control. They will befriend you, do all of the necessary things to be trusted, so they can gather information. This is the epitome of two-faced deceit. Like the tactics of politics in coup's conducted by the C.I.A we are now faced with the same tactics on the individual. On the job, in your email & social media, in your spending, banking, religion, travel, this book LOL...all the intimacies of your life are constantly being subjected to search & gathering to use against you.

So, if by chance you happen to be like myself and my friend Maurice and you are a person who rebels and speaks his or her mind...sooner or later you may encounter some very weird interface with a person who seems to know a great deal about you but you won't know how. This plays on the fear also of being alone...being alone to stand for something you believe in, to fight or voice your opinions. More and more people are each day driven to silence by removing the carrot that dangles in front of them, or by threatening something of their livelihood etc. Like the war tactic of cutting the frontline off from its logistical supply in the rear, they will be fought until they are starved and strictned with the inability to resupply themselves. Without supplies to continue to fight and food/water the weak among them will be the first to defect to the other side. Impoverished and now looking at all that tempts them in ending their hunger they will do or offer just about anything... One of the oldest tactics; just so happens to work... It works on the flip side of the coin to, when you give someone who has had very little in life something of comfort, privilege, wealth, they will do or say just about anything to maintain it. This type of corruption has been what has placed leaders in control of countries, used to infiltrate organizations both private and public, as well as religions. What does this say about people today? To me it tells me that all the integrity and the best characteristics of people are for sale. I can remember when I was a kid, snitching was a death penalty...but today it's a career. Even within our own family structures the bonds of loyalty through blood DON'T EXIST...people compete, and exercise every type of jealousy there is. For a Muslim a persons person, property, blood and honor are sacred...if and when I say a'salaamu alaykum or respond with wa alaykum salaamu I am not just saying peace unto you...I'm in fact telling this person in wishing peace onto you that I am not a threat to your person, property, blood (life), or your honor...This is the true meaning of the greeting, it is not merely a type of hello most people take it for. Harming a person or their property can be recompensed; but to take someone's life or to harm the honor of someone is not easily undone. The life would be indebted by your own, and the honor you sought to destroy would require all the work you did to dishonor that person to be done in rebuilding that same honor...To lightly do people consider their actions and never do they seem to realize the reciprocation of those actions back onto themselves. In my younger years I would be quick to ight; today I seek refuge with knowing that Allah holds all revenge, and thus rid myself of any anger through expression here in these words you now read. The evil people do and better yet the evil that they hide will eventually come to surface just be patient. The world we live in today is full of aspiring actors & actresses all seeking to use your information to cash in...I say why hide? Be what life intended you to be...

يَا أَيُّهَا الَّذِينَ آمَنُوا لَا تَتَّخِذُوا بِطَانَةً مِنْ دُونِكُمْ لَا يَأْلُونَكُمْ خَبَالًا وَدُّوا مَا عَنِتُّمْ قَدْ بَدَتِ الْبَغْضَاءُ مِنْ أَفْوَاهِهِمْ وَمَا تُخْفِي صُدُورُهُمْ أَكْبَرُ ۚ قَدْ بَيَّنَّا لَكُمُ الْآيَاتِ ۖ إِنْ كُنْتُمْ تَعْقِلُونَ

O YOU who have attained to faith! Do not take for your bosom-friends people who are not of your kind. They spare no effort to corrupt you; they would love to see you in distress. Vehement hatred has already come into the open from out of their mouths, but what their hearts conceal is yet worse. We have indeed made the signs [thereof] clear unto you, if you would but use your reason. *The verses continue in 119-120:* Lo! You are the ones who love them but they love you not, and you believe in all the Scriptures. And when they meet you, they say, "We believe." But when they are alone, they bite their nails at you in rage. Say: "Perish in your rage. Certainly, Allah knows what is in the breasts (all the secrets). "

3:120 If a good befalls you, it grieves them, but if some evil overtakes you, they rejoice at it. But if you remain patient and have Taqwa (remain with a consciousness of Allah, continuing in good deeds and behavior), not the least harm will their cunning do to you. Surely, Allah surrounds all that they do. *Quran surah al-Imran verses 118-120*

<u>Heart</u>

It takes a weak heart to judge...and with that statement I want to set the stage of this chapter towards speaking to that...In all of our capacities and abilities bestowed on us individually by the creator we are all equal but unequal in ability; only in ways of justice and rights are we considered with equality; however because we are not equal in ability nor do we have the same rights of justice life is now extremely unbalanced to say the least...

I have never been a follower, and never afraid to be the loner type...but I am actually afraid all the time... In travel, in profession, in life and even with sharing my thoughts and ideas with you in this book. But each time I challenge the fear and use it to aid me and not prohibit me, I get better with accepting what comes with it.

As the world shrinks with technology, politics, and religion... We are now constantly looking into fearful moments; dishonest people who won't think twice about serving their own interest... But this isn't only about pointing out the bad character in others... This is also about you and I. Like the boxer in the 10th, 11th, and 12th rounds whose behind in points we have to dig deep into ourselves to strive hard. These are the days that test men souls, I know someone is known for having said that, but I don't recall who... Struggle will either bring out the best in you or the worst in you.

And technology is proving to making us worse yet. Yes, in many ways we have benefited from electricity, refrigeration, washing machines and architecture that all make life more easy and comfortable, but for everything that has brought benefit we have 10 that bring destruction...Technology in this sense robs us of our intelligence, our freedoms, and natural inclinations... But many would argue otherwise. Yes in some regards it's very beneficial but has every application of technology been give the litmus test of what the consequences will be after it is manifested into daily use? Automobiles destroy the environment while they also use other mass quantities of resources just to operate so you and I can say we have the liberty of transportation to drive to work and no longer need to use public transit. In addition those same resources have become items of corruption that instigate war and hoarding for control. But society's where trains are used most often the communities are overall better. To lazy now to even walk to the corner store, to the market, or to take the children to school...All the electronic type gadgets... Really since all the communication devices have come about has anyone made the connection of that to the increase of divorce as well as promiscuity? To every plus you may mention, there will be far more negatives. I'm not one advocating against technology, I'm only speaking to the negligence of it...don't we all delay children from using certain things that require responsibility to operate or acquire? So, why aren't adults also governed to some sort of standard? And why isn't society more inquisitive to their use besides just seeing dollar signs $$$? Our hearts are now in the wrong place...To selfish to understand or reason; to stubborn to learn or consider something else that is back with truth or even to ashamed to read these statements I propose. I'm not in a position to judge, nor do I...instead I'm only trying to reflect on the harshness of this world while including myself in all these thoughts. I have been very fortunate in my life...I was born into a lower middle class family and taught that hard work and life are what you make of them. I performed military service, and put myself through college twice. I worked hard at my profession and sustained a 6 figure salary for most of my career. Before more serious times in my life like now, I have dabbled my share in the world, met many celebrities and mixed with them in parties and other functions. I have traveled the world, and been to amazing places most will never see in their lifetimes but I did so not always absent of higher thought and reflection of what I was seeing...When we are young this life never has a dull moment. However, American culture has sold every generation the idea of coming about and then it will be your turn to enjoy...relationships, some of which are performing the functions of adults while still in high school, giving kids the idea that they are grown and ok to do so. But when trouble occurs parents and society always borrow the words to describing these same adolescents' has being too young and therefore they should be slapped on the wrist and not held accountable for their mistakes. We have lost the ability and the reason to govern even our own youth. Yes, I agree sometimes it's actually the case, but when we allow the youth to follow a way of life that teaches them to be unaccountable for their own mistakes we take from them a very serious lesson. I have had my fair share of trouble, but never did my parents bail me out of anything...When I was too stubborn to listen and to grown to follow the rules I left home. Leaving made reality more vivid & clear; I didn't call home for money or anything like that. I knew when my time had come to leave and so I jumped out the nest. Of course we all run into unmanageable situations and need the help from our parents, family and friends because we are all human and prone to making bad choices but even then a learning curve should be reached eventually. Never should we keep allowing the same mistakes, by re-doing the same action expecting a different outcome. You can't always throw money at problems either and expect them to go away...

The other day I spoke to an old friend after she got the email link of the last book
"**Where does the Truth Begin**"...I could tell something was wrong immediately as
she is always vibrant. So I asked, and she went onto telling me about her nephew who
was now in critical condition after being shot multiple times in the face, neck, legs, and
torso. I was shocked to hear her bad news, but more so shocked to hear why.
Apparently, he pulled into a gas station to get gas and he was wearing some designer
glasses. He got out of his vehicle and went inside to pay first. When he was exiting to
return back to his vehicle he was confronted by the gunmen to give up his glasses; but
before he could react he was shot...Then in defense of himself the gunmen kept
shooting. It's a wonder he maintained consciousness until the police arrived to describe
the man before being taken to the hospital. The story immediately took me back to my
episode of staring down the barrel of a gun pointed at me while I was robbed. Also the
same summer a friend of my cousin who I had also befriended was shot through the
chest for his car. The silliness & use of guns for material goods is completely ridiculous.
Now living in a Muslim country where guns aren't sold nor owned by the people, here
too you hear of the youth using "swords" to jack people of items of value. Just recently
the newspaper had an article showcasing a mafia type operation of more than 300
young offenders who were robbing and then selling these same items with the use of
Facebook. The hearts of people are definitely hardened, and what is the reason for it?
Well, that shrinking of the world isn't just do to technology...it's also based on other
criteria...In America there's an obvious racial, social, religious, cultural significance;
while in other places it's a deep coveting of what others have to the realization of those
who don't have. Material things, innate things that often don't enhance life, just
temporal satisfaction until you see something better. It's a trap for anyone, even those
of us who can afford them.
In all of my living I have learned a great deal about mainly myself, and by that I have
learned more about others. After my mother passed away I was then 33yrs old. I knew
something was wrong before she was even diagnosed. On one of my weekend retreats
to the country house, I noticed my mother coughing a lot when she laughed. I would
also tell her stories or share my weekly dealings with her and we would just laugh &
laugh. But I stopped short after one laugh and asked my mother when was the last
time she had a checkup? She told me maybe a year, so I suggested to her that we go
to have another. During that visit she was told she had cancer...Immediate action was
required to combat what had already become. I remember the drive home...I was
trying my best to say calming comforting words, but my mother was a SOLIDER! She

spoke but in a very calm accepting manner. She wasn't panicked and it was if she was making her peace with Allah and the sickness right then. When It came time for me to return back to the city for work the next day, I didn't want to leave her alone. Charlie my step-father had passed away not even 6mos prior and we were all still grieving from that lose. But she told me to go..."I will be ok", she told me. I called all the time, but now more so until she told me to chill out a bit and not worry so much. She was everything to me and the best friend I have ever had...she had supported me and taught me so many things; I just want to protect her. The surgery went ok, but reduced her strength...We went on walks every even after I sold the country house and bought another home near me in the city. I moved in with her to care for her and hired in home nursing to aid her when I was away during the day, and to stay with her while on business trips out of town. Then one night as she tried to go to the bathroom and I heard a very loud BOOM...Like thunder it sounded and woke me from a dead sleep in the basement where I had setup for myself somewhat of an apartment separate from the rest of the house. Then I heard a Loud Cry...it was my mother no doubt! I rushed upstairs to find her on the floor unable to move because the cancer and come back and taken briefly her motor skills of walking and balance. I felt helpless, and if cancer had a face then I would have surely beat him to death. I picked my mother up cared for her and slept next to her just looking at her with tears...My deep want for help, comfort, support...my prayers seemingly unanswered made me very upset...From this point on I can rightfully say that no one or anything mattered to me more than my mother...
After my mother passed on, I think to most people I appeared as grieving but normal...it was so far from the truth. I think I inherited this trait from her, but I was so, so close to losing it. Depression, introverted dealings with people, and seeking ways to losing myself was the norm. I worked out each morning before work as part of my routine before work, and again in the garage when I returned home in the evenings. But after the sun set each day I was left with just my thoughts, and memories. I now lived in the house she passed away in. My neighbors all friendly and highly sympathetic to my situation offered in every way imaginable. My Italian neighbor Leo and his Sicilian wife Mary cooked authentic Sicilian dishes for me all the time. My mother had won the hearts of the neighborhood when we first moved in before anyone knew she was ill. She spoke to any & every one...something I always admired about my mother her ability to communicate with anyone despite her own background of growing up in very racially motivated society. I had a very prestigious position then as an Engineer with a great company, but I didn't care anymore about my fast tracking towards management. When evaluation time came, I told my then mentor that I had loss all interest and I was

now thinking of other options. They all thought I would eventually come around in time and so they let me be...For nearly a year I came to work, sat at my desk, did my homework for university, surfed the internet exploring other consideration I was having and talked on the phone with a host of people all still emailing and checking on me. My friend Jason come to my home and he and I became very close...we still talk to this day by email. With time I regained somewhat of a normal life, but I was still deeply not happy at all. One day while cutting the grass, my other neighbor came out the house, she was an older white lady who worked as a school teacher. I normally cut her grass after cutting my own...she asked me if I was planning on staying in the home. Up until that moment I hadn't really thought much about it...it was now mine, and I had a job with nowhere else to go so I shrugged my shoulders and told her I guess so...She responded by telling me, "you bought this home for your mother, you didn't buy this house for yourself". Thinking about what she just said, she added, "You know you are young and you're smart, you have the entire world you don't need to inherit or keep this life that was not meant for you". God bless her wherever she is now...She was right! So I began to travel...I went to South Beach Miami with some friends and just contemplated what I would do. When I returned I invested in a business venture with a military friend and began traveling back and forth. I burned up all my sick time, and vacation and with nothing more to borrow from, I went back to work and resigned. They thought I was crazy, and interviewed me on why I was leaving like someone would be interviewed upon hire...I was set; I packed up and left. The business venture didn't go well in the end due to dishonest dealings of so called friends, so I broke even. My Italian neighbors had now moved but told me where and gave me the address where I would visit them often for more delicious Sicilian dishes. Now a new couple interracial and young bought the house. We became friends fairly quickly and he would try working out with me in the garage in the evenings. I told him a bit of my story, and being the case he and other friends were over for a BBQ. Still sensing I wasn't ok, they suggested I have a yard sell, to sell everything in the house. I don't know why I hadn't thought of that myself. My mother when we were kids always went to garage/yard sales for clothing my brother and I could wear to save money and preserve the nicer things we had. That being the case, they agreed to help me since the house was fully furnished. I sold everything and basically abandoned the house. Some summer nights when I couldn't sleep and had too much on my mind I would swing by there and go inside. I would sit on the hard wood floors and in the darkness just cry...look into the room where my mother laid and remember...Was I ever going to be ok? Was I ever going to stop missing her? Who would be like her to me now? My bond was extraordinary with my mother. Eventually life would take me on a 14yrs constantly traveling adventure that has now only come to a slow...

Most of those 14yrs I lived out of suit cases, with an occasion 3-6mos lease, but I never really fully unpacked anywhere I was. City to city...State to State...working just to travel again...I was still extremely lonely even when I was surrounded by people. Like after my return from the War, when the people around you haven't witnessed what you have witnessed its next to impossible for you to have a bond with them be they family or friend. Such was the case again now two fold...Most of the shallow friendships were that at best; but I did manage to meet a few people who were genuine. However those friendships were mainly based on work, and or hanging out nothing of a fulfilling gratitude. My friend Troy and I got really close and we are still close today, but now I'm more grounded in a spiritual sense while he isn't and with distance our conversations dwindle. I didn't really give much anymore towards my faith then. I prayed occasionally, but not in the manner I should nor did I read anything. I knew the bible of course and read it many times from cover to cover...I studied it a lot while in the middle-east as I was now in the land of the prophets. I understood a lot and came into knowing more...but all that had now subsided and taken a backseat to my resentment of losing my mother. I lived with an attitude, making lots of money and just living...my daughter's mother had done a good job at hindering me from seeing her at an early age, so my relationship with her was extremely hindered; I rarely called just to avoid speaking to her. Like my mother told me women who do this you really can't fight them with all the laws on their side, so just wait and when she is old enough she will find you. Mother knows best, because she did...but like most teenagers they want answers to their questions and when you tell them they don't always except. Mothers make so many sacrifices for us, we often don't hold them to blame for anything either...so my life didn't take on the meaning most lives take with children and Nomadic life doesn't afford you that luxury. I was wondering in the wilderness for 14yrs trying to find myself again...trying to find the answers to life, and what the purpose of all this birth and death is.

Eventually, I thought ok I will now try to settle again, and I land leased a brand new home...I was renting to buy on a specially made contract that didn't include interest and the owner was my boss at a new job I landed. Things seemed to be ok on the outside, but after moving in and settling a couple of months later I would begin to notice my being alone. When my mother passed she had Schnauzer #7 Megan, so I kept her and she was my only companion on the road. I talked to that dog about everything lol. It makes me laugh because she would sit with her ears at full attention; her head would turn and she would make funny facial expressions as though she understood or was trying too. If she could speak I'm sure I would've been much better...Slowing the economy forced me now to consider work again in another city, so I left keeping the house for the time being until I saw no point to return or keep it, and so I returned to sell the furnishings I had bought for the home many items I gave to the young, crazy neighbors who threw parties all the time. Besides them on occasion, being half my age now; I was always alone for the most part.

You see, we all lose people close to us but the reality is you are guaranteed to lose someone in your life that will test you...I mean test you to your core. Notice I'm not specific has to the loss of a parent? Reason for this is some people don't have the proper parent child relationship...Parents to some people are more so a friend or buddy; you are missing that wisdom that usually should come from a parent, the comfort of words that only a father or mother can give that comes from the heart, experience & love all grounded in a wisdom that lives with you. Our closest friends and relatives we miss and hold their memories dear; but when you lose someone that represents life to you, is your teacher, and helper to being a better person...Oh my God there is no words to explain the void. Jumping out of the nest to begin life is one thing, but even if you seem to know it all & have it all...I GUARANTEE YOU, you will be knocked down at the loss of this type of person. I don't say this because it's my mother, but occasionally you come across people in life that are unique, they glow with something you that you can't explain, and with them is a wisdom that is very, very deep. Things they tell you in the moment aren't understood for maybe many years, nonetheless you never forget their words. These people offer to the world something special...like that dog who has unconditional love for its owner every time they return home, these people have learned how to love, learned how to love those who hate them, learned how to love unconditionally and their words & actions are a testimony to that...
So as I have been tested with many things of my own prior, this test went on for 14yrs...I was working less now, working vigorously on projects without a break and long hours, I earned a lot of money then took months off at a time. In doing so, I returned to reading seriously but not just scripture pretty much any and everything that had to do with self-reflection, the higher self, purpose and the metaphysical. I found interesting ideas in all these writings but it would always stop short of purpose...Purpose of life, what are we here for? All these questions I had stemming from anger, I couldn't find gratification to these wants. I read one book after and another...My mother would sometimes give me a book she had read and found

interesting; she would hand it to me nonchalantly while speaking about something else and say, "here, check this one out". I would ask her about it, but she would make me read it by not telling me anything. Later I would catch her peaking around the corner to see if I was still reading it and she would smile. She understood that I too understood what she had read previously. This was fun for us because it was our searching together, and this fed our discussions. I would meditate usually after I jogged a 10mile bike trail one way; I would take in the scenery and reflect on things I had read etc. On one interesting occasion some Puerto Ricans moved into the next building mostly woman and they would see me returning from my jog sweaty and usually shirtless lol. So they would strike up small talk and eventually we get to a point where we always spoke when we saw each other as we became familiar with everyone's names. So one day, the mother invites me to their home for dinner after one of my jogs, I accepted and went home to shower. Before dinner we were all talking and she was showing me her work. She was a lecturer of history/religion and the likes and traveled often all over to deliver these lectures. She asked me my birthdate, age, year of birth etc. and pulled out all of these books of zodiac, and astronomy...she went to the pages that would identify with me and went into this deep explanation of how and why this is and how I as an individual am linked to this that and the other all with explanation. I understood for the most part because I had read a book that gave thought to this understanding. We spoke more over dinner and after dinner she invited me to go to the Indian reservation to camp out...they smoke peyote the traditional smoke of the Indian's seek spiritual enlightenment, but I wasn't really feeling that. Besides what if I smoke it and begin to freak out...I didn't know them well enough to concur, so I declined. Before I left she showed me a full size white wolf that was hanging over her bed. The canopy type bed and there was this 7-8ft wolf hanging from the top of the canopy while its tail drug the carpet, It still had the head and everything...I was stunned in the doorway. That same night, I had a dream I was on the bike trail walking and this wolf with many other dark ones were all coming toward me growling showing the teeth etc. I don't know why I didn't run in my dream, instead I just kind of moved to the side and when he lunged at me I had a sword in my hand in which I cut off his head and I woke up with heavy breathing. I didn't know the meaning of the dream then, thought it was only because I was spooked when I saw the one in her home. The next day when I saw her I told her the dream and she had a look on her face that was telling me something wasn't quite ok and that the dream may have come about by deliberate methods. She told me, which I have never forgot...she said, "You have a direct link to the creator, you should learn to live and adopt a pure life to satisfy this condition". I knew what she was saying to me meant a great deal, but I hadn't yet come to understand...Later I would understand that this type of person is a type of priestess who seeks the help of the spirit world much like that of a medium for insight or empowerment. My slaying of that wolf would be relevant to killing any magic that she tried putting on me, and my dream told her that, and this is why she left me with those words. So life went on and my searching continued.

Then New Year's Eve 2010 came, I was alone bored in my hotel...the entire day I was feeling different, Troy went back home for the holidays I myself didn't have anything at home to go back for at this point living Nomadically. The clock ticked away with the approach of evening, then later evening...nothing on television worth watching and all the noise outside of people laughing etc. I decided to shower and get dressed and take a stroll, see what's happening maybe I find something to do. I locked the door and took maybe 20 steps before something tells me to go back in the room. I didn't hear any voices, just within myself an over powering something that didn't allow me to take another step away from my door, so I returned. A little loss of breathe I sit done on the couch to catch myself, but it's as if I began to hyper-ventilate... so I took off my jacket and laid back on the bed. No sooner I lay back on the bed I feel this sort of drowsiness, and instantly I'm in a state of sleep. But the sleep wasn't deep at all, I randomly open my eyes then close and open...then I have this sensation of not being able to move at all, while in my chest I feel this incredible, incredible feeling that I can't explain to you in words. This last for maybe 30 sec or so, and when It is over I'm crying uncontrollably. Not knowing what just happened to me, I just laid there until I slept for the night. I have shared that with only one other person...I Wallahi (swear by Allah) it is the truth.

The next day, I was inclined to go to the book store and for reasons that puzzle me until this day I don't know why I was compelled but I bought my first Quran...I had read parts of it, in other books like the Gnostic Bible in which the last chapter is about Islam, but for some reason nothing had ever stuck. I went home begin reading and read the entire Quran by the end of the next day. I will spare you all the details from this point as it should be obvious. What I would like to say now with no pun intended but directed towards anyone who is born Muslim or now even a convert to Islam...Why do you not share what you know? Why do you not tell anyone about the beautiful gift you have? After reading all pain stopped, the void I had was filled and I was now on the road that would lead me to the destination in which I sought. All the wisdom taught to me by my mother, parts of other writings I had read I understood where the sources of the ideas and been derived, and there was still more...an infinite catalog of intact revelation to explain all the questions I had.

Like the boxer I mentioned earlier in the 10th, 11th, and 12th rounds having already been knocked down twice and behind on points if he wants to win, he has to dig deep into his reserves...he has to muster whatever he can in order to overcome what he is up against. 14yrs of severe pain, loss, and now searching had come to an end. I began to feel normal again and so I traveled less for the time being. But now having experienced all that I had, I began to look outside the country for residence. Slightly sickened by the society and lies I was beginning to understand I wanted no more to be a part of it. I understood that if I really want to find that place of serenity I wasn't going to find it where I was. I had friends all moving different places: Dominican Republic, Mexico, Costa Rica, and South America...but no one was looking east. I knew that these other places only foster a life style of indulging and with half naked woman surely I would NOT be able to fight that fight. I would be knocked out as soon as the plane door opened after landing...I had been all over the middle east and so it was attractive for me to consider it, besides theres the religious aspect that comes with it. Those other countries all they have is beach...the middle east has both and many of the beaches are far better.

In religion why is it that someone who has grown to fear or frown upon a man with a beard or a woman with a hijab? Aren't all the religious depictions of Christianity Jesus and Mariam all as I have mentioned? How can bad press ruin that image for everyone but without also ruining the same for your depictions? The catholic nuns of before have been taken out of their modest attire and persuaded that they now have the freedom of wearing less with modernity. But is modernity really modernity or is it a going backward in character, values, morals for man as time increases? I see it as I just asked you. In no way are we getting better...

There are many societal draw backs to being Muslim....the Muslims are the remaining target of political agendas to rid the world of belief, the Muslim identity is hated both the man & the woman, the Muslims are weak in togetherness & unity because of tyrannical leaders who aren't Muslim & western politics seeking to keeping us divided out of fear of a united Muslim Nation, the Muslims have a disorder of division based on long ago planted corruptions of nationalism which helped to destroy the last caliphate, and Muslims are currently faced with all sorts of discrimination...But the deen of Al-

Islam is the truth...so don't let the Muslims themselves or the reason we are isolated be a deterrent towards the truth...I live and will die defending those words...

WORK CITED

http://en.wikipedia.org/wiki/World_War_I

http://en.wikipedia.org/wiki/Balkan_League.

http://en.wikipedia.org/wiki/Treaty_of_London_(1913).

http://en.wikipedia.org/wiki/League_of_Nations.

www.firstworldwar.com/source/usneutrality.htm.

http://en.wikipedia.org/wiki/Xenphobia.